SUPERBASE 3

RAMSTEIN

CAUTION
Junkyard Dawg

SUPERBASE 3

RAMSTEIN

Headquarters of the USAFE

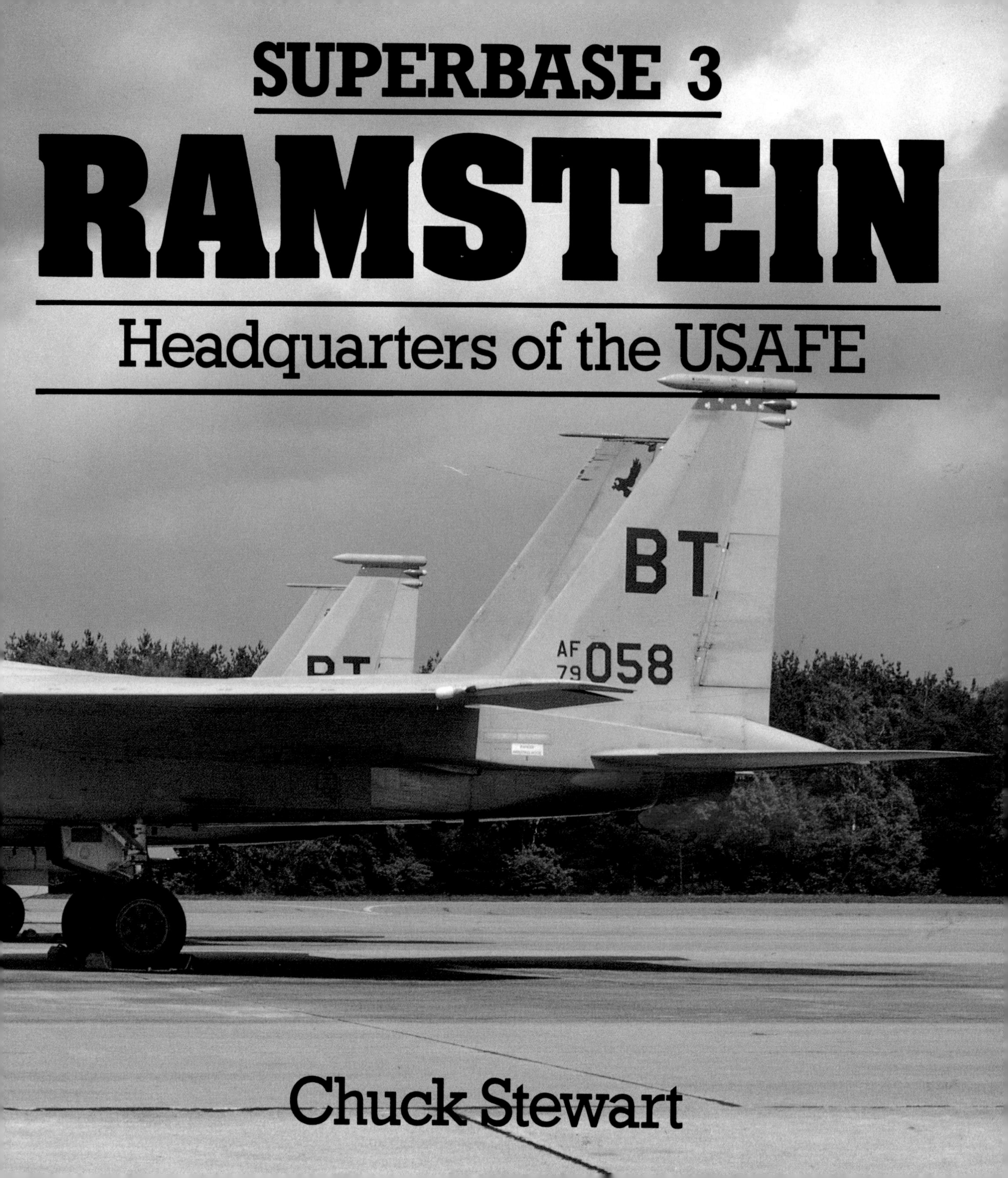

Chuck Stewart

Published in 1988 by Osprey Publishing Limited
27A Floral Street, London WC2E 9DP
Member company of the George Philip Group

British Library Cataloguing in Publication Data
Stewart, Chuck
Ramstein: headquarters of the US Air Forces in Europe.
1. North Atlantic Treaty Organization air forces. Military aircraft—Illustrations
I. Title II. Series
623.74'6'091821

ISBN 0-85045-885-4

Editor Dennis Baldry
Designed by David Tarbutt
Printed in Hong Kong

Front cover Beautifully marked General Dynamics F-16C Fighting Falcon flown by the commander of the 526th Tactical Fighter Squadron at Ramstein. (See also 'Resident Falcons', chapter one)

Title pages A McDonnell Douglas F-15C Eagle from the 525th Tactical Fighter Squadron, 36th Tactical Fighter Wing, based at Bitburg. This aircraft carries the barely-noticeable nickname *Junkyard Dawg* on the engine inlet

To my father, who taught me a love of airplanes, and my mother, who loves us both anyway.

The 86th TFW 'mascot' in front of Base Ops reflects the changing times. On the left, a model of 'Peppermint Patty,' the Wing King's candy-striped F-16, popular symbol of Ramstein since 1985. On the right, the new look of the 86th, introduced following the first of two changes of command in 1987

Introduction

Immediately after WW 2, construction began on a NATO airbase to be situated alongside the autobahn that separated the rural German villages of Ramstein and Landstuhl near the southwest German border with France. In 1953, the project was completed, resulting in not one, but two bases: Ramstein Air Base on the north side of the runway, and Landstuhl Air Base on the south side. Consolidated into the largest NATO airbase in Europe in December 1957, the two bases became Ramstein/Landstuhl Air Base. But over time, this was shortened to simply Ramstein Air Base, its present name.

Since it was activated in January 1953, Ramstein has twice been home to the 86th Tactical Fighter Wing. Their first stay, as the 86th Fighter Bomber Wing, flying F-84Fs, then as the 86th Fighter Interceptor Wing, flying F-86Ds, lasted until October 1966. At that time, the 86th TFW was moved to nearby Zweibrucken Air Base to make room for the 26th Tactical Reconnaissance Wing and its RF-4Cs, newly arrived from NATO-hostile France. The 86th's present stay at Ramstein began in January 1973, when they returned as the 86th Tactical Fighter Wing flying F-4E Phantom IIs. In late 1985 they began a conversion to the F-16 Fighting Falcon, their current mount.

Today, as headquarters of the US Air Force in Europe (USAFE) and the Allied Air Forces Central Europe (AAFCE), Ramstein has perhaps the busiest, most interesting transient ramp of any base in Europe. It is here, during a period of 15 months—December 1986 through February 1988—that all the photographs in this book were taken. It would be impossible to include every interesting aircraft that visited Ramstein during that time, so only a representative sampling of the most-interesting types and colour schemes, taken under the best possible conditions, is presented here. Alas, the RAF Hunter T.7, the Finnish F.27, the Turkish C-130 and numerous others that showed up in the rain, are not included. That all those included in the book were photographed under sunny skies during perhaps the worst year of European weather in decades is testimony to the author's patience and persistence, to say nothing of sheer good fortune.

Chuck Stewart is a highly-respected aviation photographer and historian from California whose work has appeared in numerous publications. He uses a Nikon F-3 camera, Nikon lenses and Kodachrome 64 film exclusively. He would like to thank Dietmar Letterman, a good friend and fellow aviation enthusiast, for his invaluable assistance in verifying facts for this book. And thanks as well to the unsung heroes on the transient ramp, without whose cooperation many of the photos in this book would have been impossible.

Contents

Introduction

1 Resident Falcons

2 Resident transports

3 Battle damage repair

4 Zweibrucken Phantoms

5 Spang Weasels

6 Hahn Falcons

7 Sembach Hercules

8 CIA 737s

9 Lakenheath Aardvarks

10 Bentwaters' Warthogs

11 Torrejon Falcon

12 Keflavik Eagle

13 Army visitors

14 'Happy Hooligan'

15 Seymour-Johnson Phantoms

16 Transports and tankers

17 First B-52 in Germany

18 German visitors

19 French visitors

20 Belgian visitors

21 RAF visitors

22 Dutch visitors

23 Danish Drakens

24 Norwegian visitors

25 Italian visitors

26 Canadian visitors

27 Egyptian visitors

28 Pakistani Hercules

29 Turkish Starfighter

Resident Falcons

Another sign of the times. The old camouflaged control tower sporting a huge F-4 silhouette was repainted during the summer to reflect Ramstein's new affiliation with the F-16

Right A green and black tail band identifies aircraft of the 512th TFS. The stylized dragon was a welcome dash of squadron *espirit de corps* added to several aircraft during the summer, but discontinued after only a few months. The 'Dragons' originated in August 1943 as a fighter-bomber squadron flying the A-20 Havoc; they have spent their entire existence since then in Europe

RS
AF
85
509

86 TFW

512TH TFS

Commanders' birds—the tale of the tails. **From top left** The black and gold lightning bolt of the 86th TFW, the black and silver dragon on German tri-colours of the 512th TFS 'Dragons,' and the red and white striped tail of the 526th TFS 'Black Knights'

Overleaf The GEC Avionics head-up display (HUD) gunsight silhouetted under an F-16's dew-covered canopy. With its well-forward cockpit and frameless, gold-tinted canopy, the F-16 offers perhaps the best visibility of any operational fighter today

Birds of a feather. Constructed of aluminium tubing and painted canvas, and mounted on caster wheels, this F-16 mockup, complete with fake serial number, was a one-of-a-kind experiment to build a cheap, expendable airfield decoy. Though it makes a fairly convincing F-16 to reconnaissance aircraft roaring over at low-level and high-speed, it was no match for satellite infra-red imagery and was abandoned in the prototype stage

F-16C of the 526th TFS commander with its cleverly-accented AF serial number in black and gold leaving no doubt as to which squadron it belongs

Overleaf The last and most attractive of the Ramstein commander birds to be painted, this F-16C, a recent transfer from Hahn, is the mount of the 526th TFS commander. The tail markings are interesting since the left side displays the squadron number, while the right side honours the 512th AMU (aircraft maintenance unit), and the AF serial (85-412) has been displaced to the ventral fin

RESCUE

512TH TFS

A trio of 526th TFS F-16Cs. Aircraft in the foreground is outfitted for the air defence role with wingtip AIM-9L Sidewinders and a centreline ALQ-131 ECM pod. Before they retired their F-4Es in 1985, the 526th had the distinction of being the last unit in the USAF operating the Phantom in the air superiority role

A pair of F-16Ds sporting the red and black tail band of the 526th TFS. The aircraft in the foreground bears the name of Maj Gen Robert Rutherford, USAFE Director of Operations, 'the flyingest general in USAFE'

Resident transports

In addition to the 86th TFW, Ramstein is also home to the 58th MAS, which provides airlift support for visiting 'brass' in the European theatre. Their well-maintained, on-call fleet includes six all-white Beechcraft C-12Fs like the above, plus C-21A Learjets and C-20A Gulfstream IIIs

40163

30502
86 EMS
TRANSIENT MAINTENANCE
2318
2319

The second of three beautiful C-20A Gulfstream IIIs to join the 58th MAS. When they arrived from Andrews AFB, Maryland, during the summer, they replaced the ageing (25-years, plus), fuel-guzzling VC-140B Jetstars

Affectionately known as 'Miss Piggy' by local spotters, this Boeing VC-135B is the star of the 58th MAS fleet. Built in Seattle in 1962, it underwent a complete overhaul in 1987 and is now back serving as the USAFE commander's personal aircraft

Inset One other flying unit calls Ramstein home—Detachment 2 of the 67th ARRS, which flies four VIP-marked Bell UH-1N Hueys in the airlift/transport role. The 67th ARRS has a second deployed unit of UH-1s, Det 9, at Zaragoza, Spain

24125
RICA

Battle damage repair

Right They also serve . . . Several retired Century Series fighters are scattered around the shelter areas at Ramstein, serving dual roles as airfield decoys and battle damage repair/maintenance training airframes. Tail markings on this F-101B hark back to prouder days with the Air National Guard's 107th FIG at Niagara Falls, New York

An ex-Greek Air Force F-102A showing the telltale signs of a battle damage repair bird. Shortly after this photo was taken, the aircraft was completely rebuilt and sprayed glossy grey. An ex-Greek F-84F in nearly mint condition received the same treatment

RESCUE

Though no other markings remain, the cartoon and nickname *Finesse* under the port intake are enough to identify this F-105F as having last flown as a 'Wild Weasel' with the 192nd TFG, Air National Guard, Sandston, Virginia

The oversprayed 'SA' tail code on this maintenance training F-4C betrays the fact that it was last flown by the 149th TFG, a Guard unit from Kelly AFB, Texas

Zweibrucken Phantoms

Right A mixed bag of RF-4Cs of the 38th TRS, 26th TRW, Zweibrucken, crowd the Ramstein transient ramp during a deployment exercise. These Phantoms fly their photo missions completely unarmed except for ECM gear and the brute getaway power of their afterburning GE J79 engines

Below European One-camouflaged RF-4C of the Zweibrucken-based 26th TRW commander in typically nose-high approach attitude on final to Ramstein's Runway 27. The defensive ECM pod is clearly visible on the port inboard wing pylon

Below right The last base operating the RF-4C in Europe, Zweibrucken received several replacement aircraft from RAF Alconbury during 1987, when the 10th TRW there began retiring its Phantoms. The freshly-painted 69-383 with the green and white diamond band of the 26th TRW, is an ex-Alconbury bird

ZR
AF
69 383

Spang Weasels

An F-4G, leading edge slots full-out, banks hard over the Eifel area north of Ramstein. Based at Spagdahlem with the 81st TFS, 52nd TFW, this Phantom is lightly armed for the Wild Weasel enemy defence suppression role with two AGM-45 Shrike anti-radiation missiles

Another Spangdahlem-based F-4G, this time from the 23rd TFS, featuring the 52nd TFW's trademark sharkmouth in subdued gray and red on the nose. The green wrap-around colours of the European One camouflage scheme are being replaced by an overall-grey air superiority scheme

Tail section of the same F-4G, showing the silhouetted Spangdahlem 'SP' tail code and the black and white tail band of the 23rd TFS

During the summer, Spangdahlem began receiving the first F-16Cs to replace its fleet of 1969-model F-4Gs. Photographed under a typically stormy German sky during a brief burst of sunshine on the occasion of its first visit to Ramstein, this F-16 sports the red and white tail band of the 480th TFS, 52nd TFW

The same aircraft back at Ramstein again in January 1988, now with a sharkmouth and eyes on the nose. Three of five USAFE fighter wings in Germany now operate the F-16, proving it to be every bit as prolific as its legendary predecessor, the F-4

Hahn Falcons

A flight of Hahn F-16Cs turns away from the F-16D photo-plane high above the overcast German Eifel. Led by the squadron commander's aircraft, these yellow tail F-16s of the 496th TFS, 50th TFW, are from the second batch (FY 84 and 85) of F-16s delivered to Hahn

HR

Close-up of *In the Mood*, named after the Glenn Miller 1940s big band anthem. Less provocative than the pin-up girls who graced Army Air Force bombers and fighters in WW 2, this relatively conservative model was hand-painted on the aircraft at the pilot's expense. Officially frowned out, but tolerated, it is one of several works of nose art carried by Hahn Falcons, in this instance an F-16C of the 496th TFS

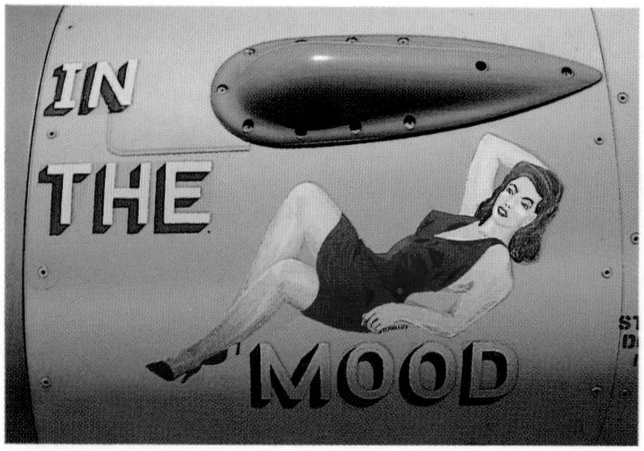

Bottom Two-seat F-16D of the 10th TFS, 50th TFW, from Hahn. The first unit in Europe to equip with the F-16, the 50th TFW removed the stylized falcon emblem, standard on later-model F-16s, from the sides of the fuselage and added a larger, more realistic falcon to the tail

IN THE MOOD
RESCUE
DO NOT PAINT
1.PUSH BUTTON TO OPEN DOOR
2.PULL RING OUT 6 FEET TO
JETTISON CANOPY
STATIC PRESSURE
DO NOT PLUG OR
DEFORM HOLES

SB
USAF
731585

Sembach Hercules

Initially operated in European-One green camouflage by the 41st Electronic Countermeasures Squadron, 552nd Airborne Warning and Control Wing at Davis-Monthan AFB, Arizona, this all-grey, antenna-bedecked EC-130H was delivered to the 43rd ECS, 66th ECW, at Sembach in mid-1987 and appeared at Ramstein for the first time during the August 'Flugtag.' The Sembach-based EC-130Hs originally began life as basic C-130H transports, but were converted for their ECM/EW role in 1981

CIA 737s

Mystery planes. Generally believed to be operated by the US Central Intelligence Agency, on the left is N99890, a Boeing 737-200/T-43A without much of a traceable history. It operated out of Rhein-Main until mid-87, when it was replaced by N57JE, a 737-204 with a less shadowy past. Caught on the ramp at Ramstein in December 1987, it wears the slightly-modified colours of its previous operator, Key Airlines of Salt Lake City, who flew it as N312XV. It may be more than coincidental that Key was a small propellor operation until it received a government contract and began jet operations from Nellis AFB, Nevada, to points in Central America in 1983. It was converted to Air Force T-43 standards for use by the CIA

N57JE

Lakenheath Aardvarks

An F-111F of the 494th TFS, 48th TFW, RAF Lakenheath, wearing the standard aft-centreline ECM pod and patriotic post-Libya nose art. Though its service introduction in 1967 was a well-publicized fiasco due to a number of design flaws that had not been worked out before delivery, more than 500 swing-wing F-111s were eventually built, including 106 F-models like *Miss Liberty*

LN
AF
70
416

Bentwaters' Warthogs

The multi-coloured tail band and silhouetted 'WR' tail code identify this A-10A as the mount of the 81st TFW commander from RAF Bentwaters. The largest fighter (attack) wing in the Air Force, the 81st TFW consists of six squadrons, some 100 A-10s, based at both RAF Bentwaters and RAF Woodbridge

WR
81ST TFW
AF 81 981

Standard A-10 armament is the 7-barrel, 30 mm GAU-8/A Avenger cannon. The 81st TFW commander's bird sports one with a difference: a chrome-plated barrel

Though officially designated 'Thunderbolt II,' the A-10 is more commonly referred to as 'Warthog' for its ability to root around in the mud destroying enemy tanks. The inside of the access panel for the A-10's built-in step-ladder is the standard location for forbidden Warthog nose art. The 81st wing king's aircraft features a typical gun-toting warthog caricature; plus the colours of the six 81st squadrons; the USAFE motto, 'Right people, right mission, right now;' and the commander's nickname, *Boss Hog*

The 81st TFW consists of six squadrons of A-10s: the 78th and 91st at RAF Woodbridge, and the 92nd, 509th, 510th and 511th TFS at RAF Bentwaters. Each squadron periodically rotates 8 aircraft to detachments deployed at one of four forward operating locations in Germany. Det 1 is located at Sembach, Det 2 at Leipheim, Det 3 at Ahlhorn, and Det 4 at Norvenich. This thumbs-up comes from the pilot of a 92nd TFS A-10 operating with Det 3 at Ahlhorn

Torrejon Falcon

El Conquistador, the spectacularly marked F-16A of the 401st TFW commander at Torrejon, Spain, pays a visit to Ramstein in March 1987. Perhaps symbolic of the recent Spanish government decision to close Torrejon Air Base, resulting in the deactivation of the 401st, its splendour was short-lived. When it returned to Ramstein in January 1988, *El Conquistador* had been stripped of its special markings and returned to duty as just plain 82-977

Keflavik Eagle

Though by definition based in Europe, this F-15D is nonetheless a long way from home. The 'IS' tail code and checkerboard band identify it as an F-15 of the 57th FIS based at Naval Station Keflavik, Iceland, and famous for its intercepts of Soviet *Bears* and *Badgers* on patrol over the North Atlantic. The long-range missions of their F-15Ds are made possible by the addition of CFT-packs, low-drag, conformal fuel tanks fitted against the sides of the fuselage, carrying target-sensing electronics and an additional 9700 lbs of fuel each

Sra Chris Metzger
RESCUE
977

Army visitors

The lack of a profusion of antennas indicates this black-cowled Army U-21A King Air of the 56th Aviation Company, Vicenza, Italy, is used in the utility transport role rather than for electronic reconnaissance as are many Army twins in Europe

Just a plain-looking olive-drab Army Huey on the outside, this UH-1H from the 25th AC, Stuttgart, offers a pleasant surprise to passengers. Instead of the usual canvas sling seats, this VIP transport is equipped with padded red velvet seats. In the end, small consolation, since the UH-1's infamous eggbeater effect has never been effectively dampened

'Happy Hooligan'

When Ramstein's 86th TFW began conversion training for the F-16 in late 1985, they had to surrender their 'Zulu' alert interceptor mission along with their F-4Es. F-15s at Bitburg took up some of the slack, but it fell to stateside Air National Guard units to fulfill the rest of the committment. For nearly $1\frac{1}{2}$ years, F-4Ds from Guard units in California (Fresno, 144th FIW), Minnesota (Duluth, 148th FIG) and North Dakota (Fargo, 119th FIG) rotated to Ramstein to stand Zulu alert. Whenever unidentified aircraft strayed into the West German ADIZ, the heavily-armed F-4s were scrambled from their alert hangars to intercept and turn back the bogey. An F-4D of the 119th FIG 'Happy Hooligans,' North Dakota ANG, returns to Ramstein from an intercept carrying typical Zulu armament: four AIM-7 Sparrows, four AIM-9 Sidewinders and a 20 mm M61 Gatling gun on a centreline pod

THE Happy Hooligans
40968
17

335TH TAC FTR SQDN
CHIEFS
ARMAMENT

RESCUE

Seymour-Johnson Phantoms

Visiting Ramstein during a weekend cross-country, F-4Es of the 4th TFW, Seymour-Johnson AFB, North Carolina, were operating out of Witmundhaven as part of a squadron exchange with JG-71 'Richtofen,' a German Air Force wing also flying F-4s. 4th TFW commander's Phantom wearing the squadron emblem of the 334th TFS 'Eagles'

Inset Pilots and WSOs confer before pre-flighting their 335th TFS F-4Es. They are wearing JG-71 'Richtofen' patches on their flight suits, souvenirs of their squadron exchange

Transports and tankers

Below Designated the C-22B, this is one of four ex-airline Boeing 727s recently acquired and modified for operational airlift support missions by the New York Air Guard. 34612 paid several visits to Ramstein, hauling Reservists to and from their annual summer encampment

Bottom right A freshly-painted 1960-model KC-135Q of the 380th Bomb Wing, a composite SAC unit consisting of KC-135s and FB-111As, from Plattsburgh AFB, New York. Stateside KC-135s regularly rotate to RAF Mildenhall and RAF Fairford to perform aerial refuelling missions for USAF and NATO aircraft throughout the European theatre. But in the case of 00335, not just any aircraft. One of a handful of internally-modified 135Qs, it carries the special JP-7 fuel used by only one aircraft in the world, the Beale, Kadena and Mildenhall-based SR-71

Right One of some 732 delivered to the Air Force, this 30-year old Stratotanker from the 145th ARS, 160th ARG, at Rickenbacker ANG Base, Ohio, was re-engined with more-powerful JT3D engines from retired 707 airliners. Now designated the KC-135E, it is one of 128 KC-135A tankers upgraded for the ANG and AFRES

80017
OHIO AIR GUARD
U.S. AIR FORCE

Plattsburgh
00335
U.S. AIR FORCE

00376

This all-white C-135E VIP transport of the 8th TDCS carried Secretary of the Air Force Edward Aldridge to Ramstein in June 1987 for meetings with the USAFE commander

First B-52 in Germany

The Eighth Air Force comes to Germany. A significant event in German aviation and political history occured on 5 August 1987 when the first B-52 ever to land on German soil arrived at Ramstein for static display at 'Flugtag,' the annual base open house. That 'historic' aircraft was 92601, a short-tail B-52G of the 40th AD, 416th BW, at Griffiss AFB, New York, resplendent in new camouflage and Statue of Liberty tail markings. It is one of some 190 G-model 'BUFFs' currently in the SAC inventory

GRIFFISS
GRIFFISS

HINTERER PILOT
SCHEIBE EINDRÜCKEN
GRIFF ZIEHEN
REAR PILOT
BREAK GLASS
PULL HANDLE
DANGER - GEFAHR
SCHLEUDERSITZ
EJECTION
SEAT
DANGER - GEFAHR
DANGER - GEFAHR
41
VORDERER PILOT
SCHEIBE EINDRÜCKEN
GRIFF ZIEHEN
FORWARD PILOT
BREAK GLASS
PULL HANDLE

German visitors

The pilot of a JBG-49 Alpha Jet from Furstenfeldbruck catches one last fresh breeze while waiting for the ground crew to pull chocks. *Luftwaffe* Alpha Jets entered service in 1978 and are equipped with Stencel-type ejection seats manufactured by Masserschmitt-Bolkow-Blohm (MBB)

An Alpha Jet of JBG-41, Husum, freshly-painted in the *Luftwaffe's* new wrap-around green camouflage scheme. In the background, an F-111F of the 494th TFS, RAF Lakenheath

Below Nearing the end of a long career, this TF-104G has been transferred from JBG-34 to LVR-1, an unusual technical/supply unit operating from Erding. Part of its mission is to provide F-104 proficiency time for older pilots with too little time remaining in service to make transition to the Tornado economically feasible. Although the tail emblem is unidentified and probably of local origin, the pilot wears the distinctive winged-gear emblem of LVR-1 on his helmet

Right The tail of this Alpha Jet tells quite a story in a glance. In addition to the aircraft type and serial number (0172) under the German flag and the squadron crest of JBG-41, the markings in white commemorate this aircraft's participation in 'GAFTIC-84,' a deployment by JBG-41 and 43 to Goose Bay in Newfoundland, Canada. Reaching the location of their 'German Air Force Training in Canada' involved a rather epic flight via England, Iceland and Greenland

LUFTWAFFE-ALPHA JET-0172
GAFTIC 84
GOOSE BAY
JABOG 43
JABOG 41

A Panavia Tornado from German Navy Flying Wing 2 at Eggebeck taxies out after the 'Flugtag.' The Tornado was designed and built jointly by British Aerospace, MBB and Aeritalia specifically for the tri-national requirement for a multo-role combat aircraft. This Tornado, in the Navy's latest camouflage, is appropriately armed for the naval interdiction/strike role with two 27 mm cannons in the nose and Kormoran anti-ship missiles

An unusual VFW-614 from the *Luftwaffe's* VIP transport and liaison wing, known simply as FBS, based at Cologne/Bonn airport. One of the few designs in the world to feature jet engines mounted above the wing, it demonstrates, along with the HFB-320 Hansa Jet, the *Luftwaffe's* penchant for innovative executive transports

58 54

58 59

Left The *Luftwaffe* bought 101 of these rugged Do-28D-2 STOL Skyservants and equipped each of its wings with four for light transport and liaison duties. This one, in the older-style camouflage with large buzz numbers and insignia, is from AKG-51 at Bremgarten

Bottom left This Do-28D-2 of JBG-34 at Memmingen displays the new-style camouflage. The nickname *Allgau Express* on the engine cowling refers to this Skyservant's home base, the Allgau region of Bavaria

Below The all-white livery and blue cheatline identify this Do-28D-2 as one from the VIP transport wing at Cologne/Bonn

French visitors

Below Looking as shiny and fit as it did when it came off the production line nearly 30 years ago, this Morane-Saulnier MS.760 Paris from ET-1/65, Air Transport Command, at Villacoublay is used for short-distance liaison flights

Bottom A Dassault-Breguet Mirage IIIE, from EC-1/13, SPA-100, 'Artois,' based at Colmar. As stenciled on the centre of the fuselage, the Mirage is powered by a single SNECMA Atar 9C afterburning engine that gives it Mach 2 capability

Right Mirage pilots have tremendous *espirit de corps* and many pay out of their own pockets to have their flying helmets personalized with beautifully-rendered artwork based on their squadron emblem or some other patriotic theme. Resting on the cockpit ledge of a 13 Wing Mirage from Colmar, this typically colourful helmet features a formation of Mirages over the Alps

The Mirage 5 was designed to fulfill an Israeli Air Force requirement for a clear-weather fighter-bomber with greater range than the standard Mirage III. Though Israel placed orders for 50 of the first production batch, for political reasons the aircraft were never delivered and were drafted into French Air Force service. This freshly-painted Mirage 5F of EC-3/13, SPA-85, 'Auvergne,' at Colmar is one of the aircraft originally built for Israel

A Mirage III sits on a rain-soaked Ramstein ramp

Another masterpiece by 'Titou,' who seems to have painted most of the personalized helmets used by Mirage pilots from 13 Wing at Colmar. In this case, the helmet of flying officer Armando of EC-3/13

Jointly-built by British Aerospace and Aérospatiale of France, the SEPECAT Jaguar above is the single-seat A-model attack version built for the French Air Force. An aircraft from EC-3/11, SPA-69, 'Corse,' at Toul-Rosieres, the well-worn desert camouflage reflects a tour of combat duty in Africa, where the French are conducting strike operations against Polisario guerilla forces in Chad from bases in Senegal and Mauritania. In addition to bombs or rockets carried on underwing pylons, French Jaguars are armed with two 30 mm DEFA cannons in the fuselage

Belgian visitors

Because of their close proximity, Belgian Air Force aircraft of all types are the most common visitors to Ramstein. This SIAI-Marchetti SF.260M elementary trainer is wearing standard orange training markings and the penguin emblem of 5 Sqn at Goetsenhoven

Close-up of ST-11's colourful sharkmouth nose and anti-birdstrike spinner. The Belgian Air Force operates 31 SF.260Ms in three training squadrons

A Dassault-Breguet Mystere 20 glows brilliantly against a black storm sky. Known as the Falcon 20 in the US, CM-01 is one of two Mysteres operated by the Belgian Air Force VIP transport squadron, *Smaldeel* 21

One of six Swearingen Merlin IIIAs operated by 21 Sqn, 15 Transport and Communications Wing, on VIP transport and liaison missions from its home base at Melsbroek

MT35

MT 48
MT48

Left With the exception of the Piper Super Cub glider tug, the oldest aircraft in the Belgian inventory is the Fouga (later Potez, and finally, Aérospatiale) Magister CM-170, first delivered in 1956. MT-35 is a well-maintained example in standard aluminium finish from 7 Sqn, Brustem

Bottom left Proof that the Magister is a rugged, fully aerobatic trainer is MT-48, still wearing the all-red livery of the Belgian Air Force aerobatic team, the long-disbanded 'Diables Rouges.' Flying out of 9 Sqn at Brustem with several other ex-Red Devils Magisters, MT-48 paid a visit to Ramstein in November 1987

Below Licence-built by SABCA/Fairey at Gosselies, Belgium since 1978, the F-16 has rapidly become the star of Belgium's fighter-bomber force. This F-16A is from 13 Sqn, 10 fighter-bomber wing, at Kleine-Brogel

RESCUE

Obviously, French Mirage pilots haven't cornered the market in flashy flying helmets, as this tiger-striped F-16 pilot demonstrates

RAF visitors

RAF visitors to Ramstein were an infrequent but always interesting lot. For example, this red and white BAC Jet Provost T.5A from No 1 Flying Training School, Linton-on-Ouse, managed the trip without a wingman

An overall-grey air defence Phantom FGR.2 of No 56 Sqn from Wattisham. A highly-modified version of the US F-4M, the RAF FGR.2 is powered by twin Rolls-Royce Spey turbofan engines

Originally designed for the Royal Navy, the rugged and reliable Hawker-Siddeley Buccaneer entered RAF service in 1969, specializing in low-level interdiction. Together with No 12 Sqn, the Buccaneers of No 208 Sqn operate from their base at Lossiemouth, Scotland, in the maritime strike role. This S.2B serves with No 12 Sqn

XW917 is a Harrier GR.3, from No 3 Sqn based at Gütersloh, Germany as part of the UK's strike and support contribution to the NATO 2nd Allied Tactical Air Force. The GR.3 is the standard version of the Harrier in RAF service today, featuring a nose-mounted laser-ranger and marked target-seeker (LRMTS) that helps make it such a superb close-support ground-attack aircraft

109
XV109

A classic design from the late-fifties, the Vickers VC10 was the world's first intercontinental-range jet transport to employ the rear-engine, clean-wing concept. Most remaining in RAF service are converted airliners used by No 101 Sqn as aerial tankers and are designated VC10 K.2. However, nine long-range transport versions like this VC10 C.1 remain in service with No 10 Sqn at RAF Brize Norton in Oxfordshire

Dutch visitors

Below A Fokker-built NF-5A of 314 Sqn, Eindhoven, in the Royal Netherlands Air Force's new overall-grey tactical camouflage. The Dutch use their Freedom Fighters in the close-support role

Right Close-up of Dutch NF-5A, K-3036, showing the standard armament, a pair of nose-mounted 20 mm M39A-2 cannons, each with 280 rounds

Bottom right K-3036's wingman on the flight to Ramstein was K-3033, another 314 Sqn NF-5A, in the older-style olive-drab and grey camouflage. Beneath the nose is stenciled some typical crew chief 'nose art'

033
DANGER
1. PUSH LATCH TO OPEN DOOR
2. PULL D-HANDLE OUT 6 FT
TO JETTISON CANOPY
RESCUE

K-3033
RESCUE

K-3036
TOP

The Royal Netherlands Air Force 314 Sqn badge, a yellow Sagitarius on a red circle, adorns the tails of the heavily-stenciled NF-5As

Armed with practice Sidewinders and centreline 20 mm Gatling guns, this pair of F-16As is from 306 Sqn at Volkel, a reconnaissance unit previously equipped with the RF-104G

A radar-equipped 334 Sqn F.27 medium transport. No 334 Sqn and its fleet of well-used Fokker Friendships and Troopships actually represents the entire Dutch airlift capability, as it is the air force's only transport squadron

Danish Drakens

Below This view of the single-seat S-35XD shows the side-looking camera ports along the nose, the weathered squadron badge of the 729 Esk and a freshly-applied yellow Phantom 'zap' marking, courtesy of the 334th TFS 'Eagles' from Seymour-Johnson AFB, NC

Bottom right Wingman to AR-116 for this Ramstein visit was AT-156, an Sk-35XD, the 2-seat reconnaissance version of the Draken. It is also from 729 Esk at Karup

AT-156

DANMARK

This head-on view shows to good advantage the Draken's unusual profile and high-gloss finish, two factors that, along with its licence-built Rolls-Royce Avon Mk 60 engine, help give it a top speed of 1320 mph, or Mach 2

Norwegian visitors

Along with Canada and the Netherlands, Norway is one of the major operators of the F-5 in NATO. **Right** An F-5B flown by 336 Skv from Rygge. Configured with three external fuel tanks, maximum range for an F-5 is about 1400 miles

Left Formerly equipped with 22 ex-Canadian CF-104Ds and Gs, 334 Skv at Bodo now flies F-16As. This one is armed with Sidewinders and wears the standard Norwegian Air Force camouflage

This pair of F-16As wear the blue lightning bolt and red, white and blue flying wedge of 331 Skv, sister-squadron of 334 Skv at Bodo. Having completed delivery of its order of 72 F-16s in 1986, the Norwegian Air Force has consolidated approximately 50 of its F-5 fleet into a single squadron and sold off or stored the remainder

Armed with hard-to-miss orange Sidewinders, this F-16B is also from 334 Skv at Bodo

676

The tails of two 331 Skv F-16s gleaming in the late-afternoon sunshine

9
frecce tricolori

Italian visitors

Probably the most popular and exciting aerobatic team in the world, Italy's 'Frecce Tricolori' flies a colourful and daredevil exhibition of formation and solo aerobatics that must be seen to be appreciated. Paying a visit from its home base at Rivolto, where it is part of 313th *Gruppo*, is one of the team's eleven Aermacchi MB.339s, team number 9, *Matricola Militare* serial number MM54479

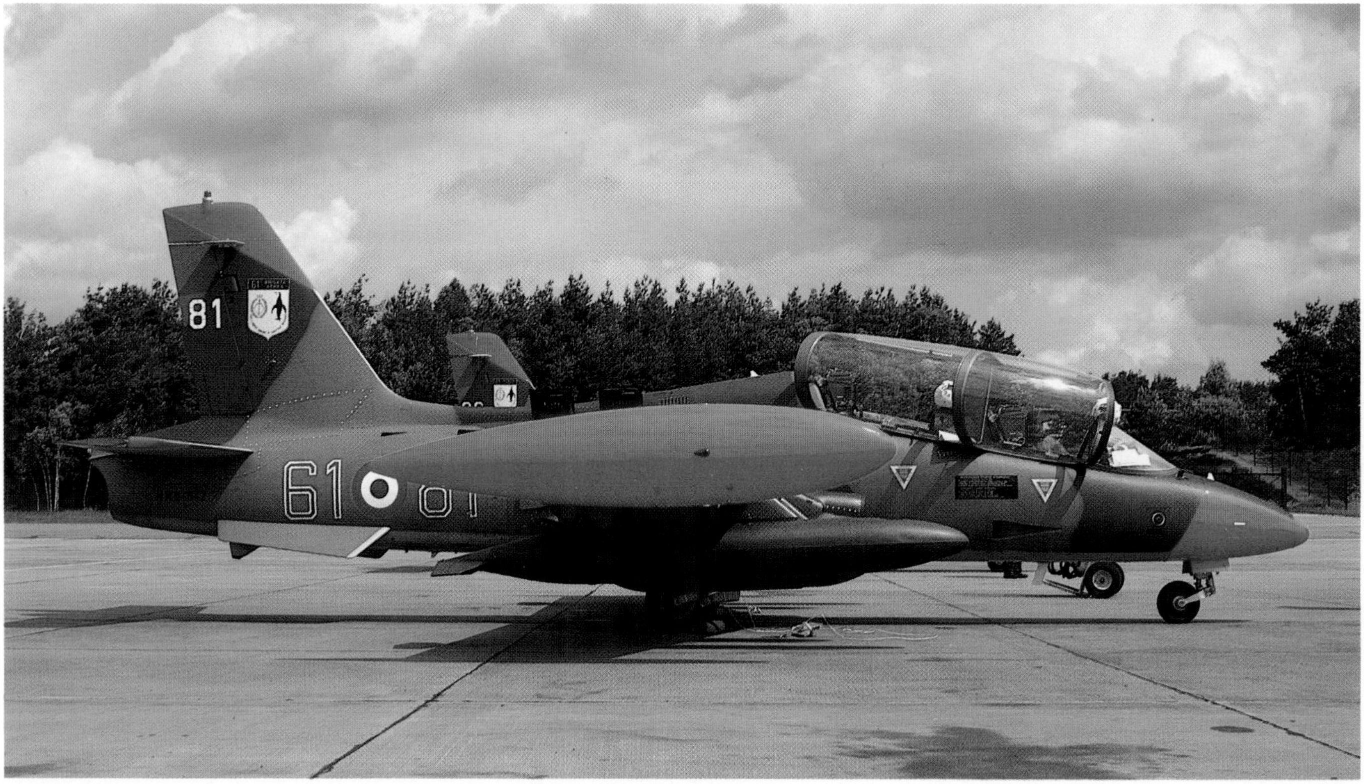

The high-visibility dayglo-orange markings on this Aermacchi MB.339K indicate it is a training aircraft. The penguin emblem of the 61st Air Brigade on the tail confirms it is from one of three squadrons assigned at Lecce-Galatina, the basic flight training base where students graduate to jets from primary training on the SIAI-Marchetti SF.260

Another Italian Air Force trainer is this 2-seat Fiat (now Aeritalia) G.91T/1, two of which visited in May 1987 from their base at Foggia-Amendola, home of the 60th *Stormo*, the air force's advanced jet training wing.

Inspired by the F-86 Sabre, the G.91 was built during the sixties as a light attack and reconnaissance aircraft, but like most successful designs, was also pressed into the fighter and trainer mold

4 10

Left The roaring-lion emblem of 20th *Gruppo*

Top left Though the massive multi-national production of the F-104 ceased in 1967, Aeritalia continued to produce an air-superiority version with a more-powerful J79-19 engine and updated radar until 1975. One of these 205 licence-built F-104Ss is shown here in the markings of the 4th *Stormo*, 9th *Gruppo*, an interceptor unit based at Grosetto

Far left The crew of a TF-104G prepares to 'button-up' for departure. Ramstein is the site of a unique phenomenon that occurs annually during November and December. Not unlike the famed return of the swallows to Capistrano, pairs of Italian F-104s swarm into Ramstein so their crews can exercise one of their NATO privileges at Europe's largest and best-stocked shopping facility, the Ramstein BX. It is not unusual to see gift-wrapped boxes of stereo components being stuffed into empty compartments and rear cockpits for the flight home to a very merry Christmas indeed

Above With the back-seater barely able to see over his haul of Christmas booty this German-built TF-104G of the 4th *Stormo*, 20th *Gruppo*, heads back home to Grosetto. Flying only 2-seaters, 20th *Gruppo* originally operated autonomously of its parent 4th *Stormo*, complete with its own '20-' identification codes. That practice was terminated in 1985 when 20th *Gruppo* also began operating single-seaters and re-marked their aircraft to conform with the standard air force coding system

Two F-104Ss wearing the mouse-killing cat emblem of the 51st *Stormo* on the tail and the pipe-smoking scarecrow 'Spauracchio' emblem of 22nd *Gruppo* on the intake at rest on a rain-soaked Ramstein ramp. The 51st *Stormo* is based at Istrana

Yet another Christmas shopper is this F-104S from the 3rd *Stormo*, 132nd *Gruppo*, at Villafranca. With its short, razorlike wings and its fuselage built around the J79-19 engine, the F-104S does not have much internal fuel capacity and normally flies with tip-tanks and under-wing tanks to give it a maximum range of nearly 1300 miles

Above One of the few German-built single-seat Starfighters remaining on the Italian Air Force rolls is this very clean F-104G, MM6563, from the 3rd *Stormo*, 28th *Gruppo*, at Villafranca

Left The flying-witch emblem of 28th *Gruppo*, the reconnaissance squadron from Verona-Villafranca

After the 6th *Stormo*, the next unit in the Italian Air Force to trade in its F-104s for the Panavia Tornado was 36th *Stormo*, based at Gioia del Colle in southern Italy. The first-ever visit of an Italian Tornado to Ramstein was made by two interceptors from that unit in February 1988. This is MM7074, with the yellow lightning bolt emblem of the 156th *Gruppo* piercing the 36th *Stormo* eagle emblem on the tail

Designed by Breguet in France and eventually licence-built in Germany, Italy and the Netherlands, the Br.1150 Atlantic was NATO's choice to replace the P-2 Neptune as its front-line maritime patrol and anti-submarine warfare aircraft. Though only 87 were built, most remain in service because of their economical 5000-mile range, 18-hour endurance and relatively inexpensive price compared to its rival, the Lockheed P-3 Orion. One of 18 Italian Navy Atlantics is this one from the 30th *Stormo*, 86th *Gruppo*, a long way from home base in Cagliari, Sardinia

Canadian visitors

Though finally (but reluctantly) retired by the USAF in early 1988 after nearly 38 years of reliable service, the T-33 basic trainer continues to fly with the Canadian Armed Forces in the form of the Canadair-built CT-133A Silver Star. A total of 6557 T-33s were built over a 10-year period, 656 being Canadair CT-133s. This example, wearing the camouflage exclusive to Germany-based Silver Stars, is from the 1st Canadian Air Group at Sollingen and is used as a proficiency trainer, liaison transport and general squadron hack

The F-18 Hornet was selected by Canada to replace its CF-101s and 104s, and as soon as the first squadrons in Canada were fully operational, conversion training began for 409 and 439 Sqns in Germany. A typically camouflaged CF-18A is this one from 409 Sqn at Sollingen. Because it is a relatively new aircraft in the European theatre, the CF-18's distinctive twin tails have more than once led jumpy ground troops to report them as MiG-25 *Foxbats*

DANGER
DANGER

Egyptian visitors

Ever since the Egyptian Air Force took delivery of some 32 F-16As, its Canadian-built DHC-5 Buffalo STOL transports have been making trips to Ramstein to pick up and deliver parts for their F-16s. SU-BFC on the transient ramp just after a winter rainstorm. During 1987, three Egyptian Buffalos visited Ramstein: SU-BFB in all-white, and SU-BFA and BFC in standard desert camouflage

SU-BFB wears a decidedly non-standard all-white livery with the Egyptian flag and air force titles on the tail, but without the usual roundel on the fuselage. Middle East military forces being the way they are, it is only an educated guess that this Buffalo is part of the Egyptian Air Force's C-130 transport unit, 16 Sqn at Cairo West

Pakistani Hercules

The Pakistani Air Force operates two squadrons of some 30 F-16s and, like Egypt, occasionally sends transports to Ramstein to pick up priority parts for its F-16s. This is a C-130E of No 6 Sqn from Peshawar, with its Islamic crew beneath the tail having just completed their afternoon prayers toward Mecca. Though it now wears the standard camouflage scheme, only six months earlier, 64144 was photographed also wearing the civil registration AP-AUT

Turkish Starfighter

Below The last country in NATO to operate large numbers of F-104s is Turkey, all of whose aircraft, except the recently-delivered F-16s, are ageing hand-me-downs from allied air forces. An example is this ex-*Luftwaffe* F-104G, which, until 1986, flew with JBG-34 as 26+04. It now flies with No 4 Wing, 142 *Filo* (squadron), a strike unit based at Balikeshir

Bottom Another ex-*Luftwaffe* Starfighter is this 2-seat TF-104G, also from 142 *Filo*. It will retain the basic *Luftwaffe* camouflage and all safety stenciling in German until its first major overhaul